DK SUPER World

CANADA

Journey through the vast country of Canada
to discover breathtaking landscapes,
diverse cultures and rich history

PRODUCED FOR DK BY
Editorial Caroline Wakeman Literary Agency
Design Collaborate Agency

Project Editor Amanda Eisenthal
Senior Art Editor Gilda Pacitti
Managing Editor Carine Tracanelli
Managing Art Editor Sarah Corcoran
Production Editor Marc Staples
Production Controller Rebecca Parton
Publisher Sarah Forbes
Managing Director, Learning Hilary Fine

First published in Great Britain in 2025
by Dorling Kindersley Limited
20 Vauxhall Bridge Road,
London SW1V 2SA

The authorised representative in the EEA is
Dorling Kindersley Verlag GmbH. Arnulfstr.
124, 80636 Munich, Germany

A CIP catalogue record for this book
is available from the British Library.
ISBN 978-0-2417-2083-7

Printed and bound in China

www.dk.com

This book was made with Forest
Stewardship Council™ certified
paper – one small step in DK's
commitment to a sustainable future.
Learn more at www.dk.com/uk/
information/sustainability

CONTENTS

Words in **bold** are explained in the glossary on page 44.

CANADA

Canada is the northernmost country of the North American continent. It's a huge land, spanning nearly 10 million square kilometres (4 million sq miles). It's so big, it has six different time zones. You'll find a lot of variety in Canada, in its people, landscapes, animals and culture.

Canada's provinces and territories

Northwest Territories

Arctic Ocean

Nunavut

Yukon

Québec

Newfoundland and Labrador

Pacific Ocean

Prince Edward Island

British Columbia

Nova Scotia

Alberta

New Brunswick

Saskatchewan

Atlantic Ocean

Ottawa

Manitoba

Ontario

FASCINATING FACT!

Canada is split into 13 regions: 10 provinces and 3 territories. Each region has its own culture, capital city, flag and even its own official bird! The official bird of Manitoba, for example, is the great grey owl.

Rocky Mountains

Fairmont Le Château Frontenac

Parliament Hill

CN Tower

Great Lakes

Niagara Falls

FACT FILE

ALL ABOUT CANADA

O Canada

National anthem

l'Unifolié

⚑ Flag: Maple Leaf (l'Unifolié)

📍 Capital city: Ottawa

👤 Population: Approx. 38.9 million

💬 Official languages: English, French

💵 Currency: Canadian dollar $

🌲 National tree: Maple

🐾 National animal: Beaver

🍴 National dish: Poutine

🎵 National anthem: "O, Canada" ("Ô Canada")

☆ Major export: Crude oil, automobiles

Cities

Ottawa in the province of Ontario is Canada's capital city. The biggest city is Toronto, also in Ontario. Toronto is home to the famous CN Tower, which is one of the tallest free-standing structures in the world, at 553 metres (1,815 ft) high.

Languages

Canada has two main official languages: French and English. This is because both countries colonised Canada in the 16th century. In the three territories, the **Indigenous** languages of Chipewyan, Cree, Gwich'in, Inuinnaqtun, Inuktitut, Inuvialuktun, North Slavey, South Slavey and Tłı̨chǫ are also officially recognised.

Halu

Bonjour

Hello

Maple syrup

Maple trees are the symbol of Canada. The maple leaf is even on the country's flag. Maple trees grow all across the land but are especially concentrated in the east, where the maple industry thrives. The syrup is made from the sap of the tree.

FIND OUT!

The national dish of Canada is poutine: fries topped with cheese and gravy. What is the national dish for your country?

POUTINE

MOUNTAINS, FORESTS AND LAKES

Canada is the second-largest country in the world. Its terrain ranges from frozen **Arctic** landscapes to vast expanses of grassland, rolling mountain ranges to luscious forests and rushing rivers.

Fitzsimmons Range mountains

Mountains

Canada is home to some world-famous **mountain ranges**, including the Appalachians, the Fitzsimmons Range and the Yukon Range. Mount Logan in the Yukon is the tallest mountain, at 5,959 metres (19,551 ft). The Canadian Rockies in the west stretch 1,600 kilometres (1,000 miles) and feed water into the Canadian **Prairies** to help maintain their **ecosystems**.

FASCINATING FACT!

Canada has the longest coastline of any country in the world, at 243,042 kilometres (151,019 miles).

Forests

Canada's **boreal forest** is an enormous area of forest and vegetation that makes up 55 per cent of all of Canada's land! The boreal forest is crucial to both **ecological** and **economic** systems. It is home to millions of animals, including rarer species like wolverines and whooping cranes. The huge expanse of vegetation also helps purify the air.

Boreal forest

Whooping crane

Lake Huron

Great Lakes

Canada has around 2 million lakes. Some of the biggest and best-known are the Great Lakes. In Canada, these are Lake Superior, Lake Ontario, Lake Huron and Lake Erie. The Great Lakes feed into river systems and provide drinking water for more than 40 million people and countless animal species.

Arctic tundra

Canada is so far north that some regions are within the Arctic Circle. There, much of the land is tundra, meaning the ground beneath the soil is permanently frozen. You won't find many trees or tall plants because of a combination of **permafrost**, strong winds, freezing temperatures and frequent winter blizzards.

FIND OUT!

The lowest temperature ever recorded worldwide was in Snag in the Yukon territory. It reached -63°C (-81.4°F). What is the coldest temperature recorded in your country?

NIAGARA FALLS

Niagara Falls is one of the most famous waterfalls in the world. But it's actually made up of three different waterfalls: the Horseshoe Falls in Canada, and the American Falls and the Bridal Veil Falls just across the border in the USA. The Horseshoe Falls is the biggest, at 57 metres (180 ft) high and 820 metres (2,700 ft) long.

FASCINATING FACT!

The water that flows over the Falls comes from the Great Lakes. Around 2,688 tonnes (3,160 tons) of water goes over the Falls every second. That's 11 Olympic-sized swimming pools per second!

Formation of the Falls

12,000 years ago, massive **glaciers** began melting and released rushing water. This water carved out the Niagara River. At some point, the river went over a cliff, and over many centuries, the water **eroded** the cliff away, creating the iconic shape of the Falls.

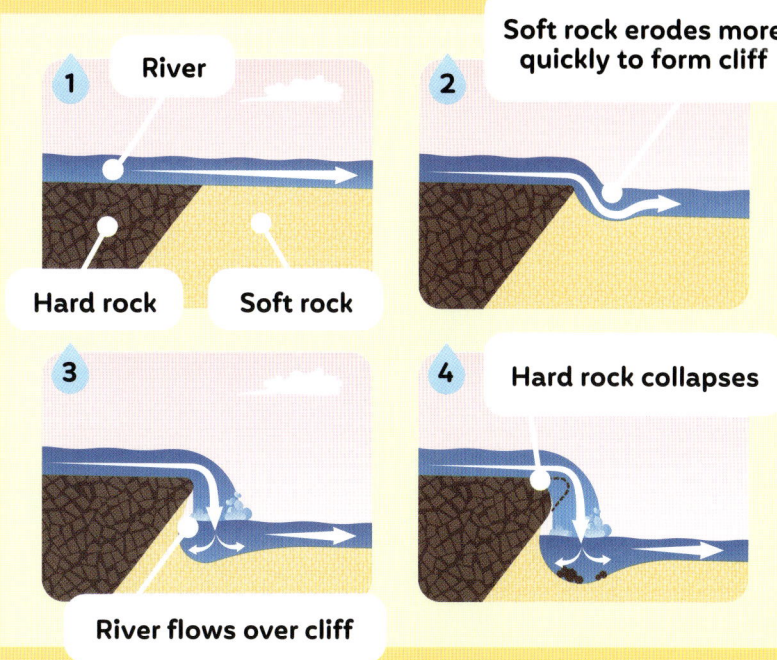

1. River

Hard rock   Soft rock

2. Soft rock erodes more quickly to form cliff

3. River flows over cliff

4. Hard rock collapses

Partially frozen Niagara Falls

Frozen Falls

Parts of the Falls freeze during winter, but there is too much water moving too quickly for them to freeze totally solid. However, they did freeze entirely in 1848 during a particularly cold March when huge ice blocks upstream slowed the flow of water. The Falls were frozen for more than 30 hours.

Daring deeds

For more than a hundred years, daredevils have been going over the Falls in barrels and various contraptions. The first person to survive such a stunt was schoolteacher Annie Edson Taylor in 1901. These days, trying to go over the Falls like this is illegal, not to mention dangerous.

FIND OUT!

The Niagara Falls is so big, it crosses the border between Canada and the USA. Can you find out which US state it crosses into?

Answer: New York State

NATURE IN THE NORTH

Many different types of animal and plant life thrive in the oceans, forests, rivers and mountains. Plants and animals are all well-adapted to their particular habitats—even the frozen ones!

SNOW DWELLERS

Polar bear

These Arctic bears are the biggest bear species in the world. Thick white fur over a layer of black skin over a layer of blubber all helps to insulate the bears against freezing temperatures. Polar bears hunt seals on the coasts and in the waters of the north.

 FASCINATING FACT!

Canada has more polar bears than anywhere else on the planet, at around 16,000 individuals. However, the sea ice they rely on is melting due to climate change and their numbers are going down.

Wolverine

Wolverines are rare members of the weasel family, but they look more like little bears. They live in the snowy mountains of the north, hunting and scavenging. The Latin name for wolverines is *gulo gulo*, which loosely translates as greedy greedy, because they'll eat frozen carcasses and bone and pretty much anything.

Snowshoe hare

Named for their large feet covered in stiff, bristly fur, snowshoe hares are adept at bounding through the snow. This helps them escape predators. In winter, they have a white coat. The winter fur sheds and turns brown through summer to act as camouflage.

Snowy owl

Snowy owls are master hunters. Their favourite prey is lemmings, but they also hunt hares, other birds and even foxes. Unlike most owls, snowy owls hunt in the day as well as at night. This is because in the Arctic Circle where they live, the Sun only sets for a short amount of time each day during the summer (and some days it doesn't set at all).

MOUNTAINS AND PRAIRIES

Rocky bighorn sheep
These sturdy sheep live in the mountain peaks of the Canadian Rockies. They are excellent climbers and can hop from tiny crag to tiny crag.

Eagle
Canada has two main species of eagle: golden eagles and bald eagles. In the mountains, they use updrafts in the air to help them soar long distances. Golden eagles are brown with lighter feathers around the neck like a lion's mane, while bald eagles have a bright white head.

Prairie crocus
These delicate purple flowers are said to tell of the start of spring. When the snow melts, the **prairie** crocuses bloom their purple, furry flowers.

Prairie rattlesnake
As the name suggests, prairie rattlesnakes live in the flat grasslands, hunting small mammals and birds using a quick strike and deadly venom. They can grow up to 1.5 metres (5 ft) long.

WATER LOVERS

Beaver

Beavers are large rodents who live in groups of 8–12, called colonies. They use their long teeth and strong jaws to gnaw down trees, out of which they build dams. The dams surround their homes with water to protect them from predators.

Orca

Also known as killer whales, orcas are very intelligent mammals. They have three different types of communication: clicks, whistles and pulses. They also work together to track and catch their prey: salmon, squid, porpoises and seals.

Atlantic puffin

These dapper birds are sometimes known as "clowns of the sea" because of their bright, multicoloured beaks. Chicks are called pufflings. They live on the sea cliffs around Newfoundland and Labrador.

Whooping crane

These cranes are the tallest birds in North America, at almost 1.5 metres (5 ft) high. They tend to nest in marshy grounds. Whooping cranes were once nearly **extinct**, and in 1941 there were only 15 left. **Conservation** efforts have helped bring their numbers up to about 800 today.

WOODLAND WILDLIFE

Boreal forest

This lush forest is populated with black and white spruce trees, which provide food and homes for squirrels, birds and more. Native aspens and willows are eaten by moose and deer, and by beavers, who also use the wood for their dams.

Moose

Moose are the largest members of the deer family. They can grow up to 3.1 metres (10 ft) long and weigh up to 600 kilograms (1,300 lb)! Moose have to eat around 30 kilograms (65 lb) of vegetation in a day to maintain their enormous bodies.

Canada lynx

These wild cats have thick fur to protect against the cold and huge paws to walk on snow. They are quick hunters and mostly prey on hares in the Canadian woodlands, but will also eat squirrels and other small mammals and birds.

Wolf

Wolves are social animals that live and hunt in close family units called packs. They mostly hunt deer, elk, wild boars and even moose. Wolves once roamed all of Canada, but as human populations spread, they retreated to wilder areas in the north.

INVASIVE SPECIES

Not all life works together. **Invasive species** can affect whole ecosystems, damaging **habitats** and reducing **biodiversity.**

Giant hogweed
This towering plant kills off other plants by blocking the Sun with its large flower head. It also has sap that harms the skin of humans and other animals.

Garlic mustard
Native to Europe, garlic mustard releases a chemical from its roots that stops other plants growing nearby. It was brought by settlers in the 1800s for food.

Purple loosestrife
It might look pretty, but purple loosestrife grows rapidly, outcompeting native plant life.

DIVERSITY, SPORTS AND ENTERTAINMENT

Canada is a country that prides itself in being **progressive** and multicultural. The nation was formed under many influences and its people continue to embrace diversity and difference. Canada's terrain and climate have a strong impact on what sports and activities are popular.

A cultural mosaic

Canada's cultural influences stem from its Indigenous roots and lasting impacts of French and British **colonisation**. The French influence is particularly strong in Québec, where French is the main language spoken. Canada also has an official policy of **multiculturalism**, which encourages immigrant communities to be part of and contribute to Canadian society.

FASCINATING FACT!

Canada's name comes from the Indigenous term Kanata, meaning "settlement" in the language of the Haudenosaunee.

Indigenous populations

About 5 per cent of the people living in Canada identify as Indigenous. Indigenous peoples live all across Canada. The largest urban **population** of Indigenous people is found in the city of Winnipeg in Manitoba. The northern territory of Nunavut is a predominantly Inuit region, and about 80 per cent of people who live there are Inuit.

The largest Indigenous populations in cities in Canada.

Vancouver

Edmonton

Saskatoon

Ottawa-Gatineau

Winnipeg

Montréal

Calgary

Regina

Halifax

Toronto

Different peoples

There are three broad categories of Indigenous peoples in Canada: **First Nations**, **Inuit** and **Métis**. Each of these groups is made up of many nations and communities with varied cultures, customs and practices.

Customs and manners

Canadians have a reputation for being polite. Basic manners, like saying please and thank you and queueing, are valued. It's common to shake hands as a greeting, or to give a small hug if you know the person well. In Québec and other French-Canadian areas, you might see more people kiss on the cheek.

SPORTS

Hockey

Canada's official (and favourite) sport is ice hockey: a fast-paced game played on ice. Players from two teams whack a quick-moving puck around the rink with hockey sticks, with the aim of hitting it into each other's goal. Ice hockey players have to wear helmets and a lot of padding because they move so fast.

Lacrosse

Canada's other official sport is lacrosse. Two teams of ten players try to shoot a small rubber ball into the opposition's goal by throwing it to each other using sticks with nets. Lacrosse is based on an Indigenous game called *baggataway*.

ENTERTAINMENT

Films and TV

Canada is a huge producer of films and TV, and there are strict rules on what can be considered "Canadian content". The programme or film must have Canadians as:

- The producer
- The director or scriptwriter
- At least one lead actor
- 75 per cent of all paid production and post-production staff

There is also a rule that at least 60 per cent of content played on TV must be Canadian!

Going outside

The Canadian outdoors has so much to see that you'll often find families and groups of friends going hiking, camping, swimming and kayaking. With so many mountains and lakes, it's also easy to find activities like white-water rafting, dog sledding, skiing and mountain climbing.

CHRISTIANITY AND INDIGENOUS PRACTICES

Canada is a nation made up of many peoples. Its roots lay in Indigenous cultures and European colonialism, and more modern cultural influences come from immigration and strong multiculturalism.

Christianity

The main religion of Canada is Christianity: the worship of God and his son, Jesus Christ. Christians follow the teachings of Jesus, who preached that people should be kind and treat each other as they would like to be treated. The place of worship is the church, where Christians go to pray and listen to sermons or bible readings.

Notre-Dame Basilica, Ottawa

Indigenous beliefs

Different Indigenous communities have their own systems of belief and spirituality. Some have a holy person or healer called a shaman, who might communicate with the spirits of nature, or take the role of healer, prophet or advisor. Many Indigenous peoples have also adopted Christianity, sometimes alongside their traditional beliefs.

Powwows

A modern powwow is a meeting of people from different Indigenous cultures. It is a celebration to share food, music, dancing, drumming and crafts.

Storytelling

Storytelling is a strong practice among Indigenous peoples. Some groups have a creation story that centres on a hero or animal who dives into deep water to bring back mud, which is then made into the Earth. Other communities like the Haudenosaunee say that the world is carried on the back of a giant turtle. This is why many Indigenous peoples use the term Turtle Island to refer to North America.

Other beliefs

More than a quarter of Canadians consider themselves secular, which means they have no religious belief. Canada is a diverse nation with many communities of different cultures, so there are many religions too. Around 5 per cent of the population are Muslim, and there are significant numbers of Sikh, Buddhist, Hindu and Jewish followers.

CELEBRATIONS

On public holidays, schools and workplaces are often closed. Some holidays are nation-wide and some are decided by provinces. While many holidays and festivals have Christian roots, they are often enjoyed by everyone.

National Indigenous Peoples Day (Journée nationale des peuples autochtones)

This day celebrates Indigenous heritage and culture. It is held on 21 June because the summer solstice – the longest day of the year – in mid-June is important in many Indigenous cultures. Celebrations include storytelling, music, food, art and dance.

Canada Day (Fête du Canada)

Canada Day on 1 July marks the anniversary of the Canadian Confederation, which helped Canada unite as a country. This is a patriotic holiday celebrated with fireworks, barbecues, flags and parades.

FASCINATING FACT!

Did you know that Santa has an official address in Canada?
Santa Claus
North Pole
HOH OHO
Canada

for Santa C.
North Pole
Planet Earth
Milky Way Galaxy

Thanksgiving
(Action de grâce)

On the second Monday of October, people get together to give thanks and enjoy a meal of turkey or fish, vegetables, potatoes and gravy. Thanksgiving began in 1578 when English explorer Martin Frobisher landed in Newfoundland and threw a feast to give thanks for a safe voyage.

Christmas
(Noël)

Christmas is the big holiday for many people in Canada. On 25 December, families and friends give presents and eat a feast, and Santa Claus brings gifts to children in the night. In some provinces, the day after Christmas is Boxing Day, and people watch ice hockey or take advantage of sales.

Québec Winter Carnival
(Carnaval de Québec)

This is one of the world's largest winter festivals! There are parades, snow sculptures, ice skating, sleigh races and lots of fun! There is also a full-sized palace made entirely from ice. It goes on for two weeks at the end of January.

CANADIAN CUISINE

Many dishes in Canada have British and French influences, but often with a unique Canadian twist.

Maple syrup

You can't talk about Canadian food without talking about maple syrup, made from the sap of maple trees. It is enjoyed with pancakes, waffles and French toast; made into hard sweets and ice creams; and even drizzled over roasted vegetables and meats.

Poutine

Canada's national dish is poutine: french fries topped with cheese and smothered in hot gravy. Poutine is a comfort food and is often eaten at celebrations and fairs. It is a uniquely Canadian invention, and first emerged in the 1950s in Québec, where it is particularly popular. There are even poutine festivals!

Poutine

FASCINATING FACT!

It takes 40 litres (10.5 gallons) of maple sap to create just one litre of maple syrup!

Coffee

The drink of the nation is coffee! There is no particular way Canadians prefer their coffee, except in large amounts.

Butter tarts

These are pies made with flaky pastry and filled with a sweet mixture of butter, sugar, maple or corn syrup and egg. Some say butter tarts evolved from a French recipe. Others argue that it has Scottish origins. Whichever is true, it is now thoroughly Canadian!

Poor man's pudding (Pouding chômeur)

This dessert is a **Québécois** comfort food staple, made from a simple cake batter poached in maple syrup. It was invented during the Great Depression in the 1930s when there were not a lot of rich ingredients to use.

Lobster rolls

These are buttery hot dog rolls filled with lobster and mayonnaise and served cold. Lobster rolls are common in Nova Scotia, where lobster is so abundant it used to be called "poor man's food".

Juice

Fruit juice is the second favourite drink in Canada, after coffee. Orange and apple juice are the top flavours, but there is also a uniquely Canadian juice made of tomatoes and... clams!

BUTTER TARTS

Butter tarts are warm and gooey treats! There are many variations of butter tart. In this one, we use raisins and pecans, but some people prefer maple syrup and walnuts—or even chocolate chips for a nut-free version. This recipe makes 12 tarts.

PASTRY

Ingredients

- 200 g (1 $\frac{2}{3}$ cups) of plain flour
- 100 g (7 tbsp) of unsalted butter (chilled and cut into small cubes)
- 1 egg
- ¼ tsp of salt

Method

1. Start by making the pastry shells. In a big bowl, stir the salt into the flour.
2. Add the butter and rub the flour and butter between your fingers until it looks like breadcrumbs.
3. Mix in the egg to form a smooth dough.
4. Wrap the dough tightly in cling film or a reusable wax wrap and put it in the fridge for 30 minutes.
5. After 30 minutes, roll the dough out and use a 10-centimetre (4 in) cookie cutter or similar sized cup to cut out the individual tarts.
6. Grease a cupcake tin with butter and press the tarts into the holes. Next, make the filling.

Tip: If you want to skip this step, you can use shop-bought tart shells!

FILLING

Ingredients

- 150 g (¾ cup) of brown sugar
- 120 ml (½ cup) of golden syrup (or maple syrup if you prefer)
- 80 g (⅓ cup) of butter (melted)
- 2 eggs
- 1 tbsp of cider vinegar
- 1 tsp of vanilla extract
- ½ tsp of salt
- 75 g (½ cup) of chopped pecans
- 75 g (½ cup) of raisins

Method

1. Now make the filling. Preheat the oven to 190°C (375°F).
2. Whisk together the brown sugar, syrup, butter, eggs, vinegar, vanilla and salt until thick.
3. Scatter a mix of pecans and raisins (or chocolate chips) into each tart shell.
4. Pour in the filling mixture until the tart shells are about three-quarters full.
5. Bake for 20–25 minutes until the filling is golden brown and bubbling and the crusts are browning. They should puff up a little and then settle down again.
6. Let the tarts cool on a wire rack.

 Be careful not to eat too much sugar in a day. One butter tart is plenty.

LIVING AND WORKING

Where you work and what your school is like depends on whether you live in an **urban** or **rural** area. Two-thirds of the Canadian population live and work in the southern provinces, and 81 per cent live in cities.

Toronto

Working in the city

Canada has many thriving industries. The tech and computer programming sectors are strong in big cities like Toronto and Montréal. These cities, sometimes called Hollywood North, are also the centres for the Canadian film and TV industry.

Working outdoors

In the flat grasslands of the Prairies, **agriculture** is the big industry. **Renewable energy** is also a fast-growing sector, with up to 60 per cent of Canada's energy coming from **hydroelectricity**. And you won't be surprised to know that Canada is the largest **exporter** of maple syrup!

FASCINATING FACT!

Montréal has a network of underground tunnels called the Underground City that people use to avoid the extreme weather!

Going to school

Schools in Canada are mainly split into three levels:

Elementary or Primary School

Junior High or Middle School

High School

In most regions, children start school at around age 5 or 6 and graduate at 18. Many schools have lessons in both French and English. Students learn subjects like maths, science, social science, English and French and art.

Differences in provinces

Each province and territory has its own school system. That means that things like the subjects taught, whether there is a middle school, and the age students graduate can be different depending on where you live. In Québec, for example, students go straight from elementary school to high school in grade 7 and they can choose to leave at 16.

SCHOOL

RORY'S DAY

Name: Rory McIntyre-Bélanger
Age: 10
Lives: Ontario
Family: Mom, stepdad, stepsister

Hi! My name's Rory, and this is my day in 4th grade at my elementary school in Ontario. There's fresh snow in the window when I wake up, so I get dressed in warm clothes and my snow pants and go downstairs. Mom has made oatmeal for my stepsister Hanna, but I like to have cereal. It was Hanna's turn to clear the snow yesterday, so today I put my boots and my big coat on and go out to sweep the porch and steps. My stepdad walks us to school. It's cold but not snowing and we can see everyone's breath. The school bus passes with its big snow chains and I wave to my friend Carrie.

Around 8:50, we get to school and take our coats off. I go to sit at my desk as the PA crackles on and the vice-principal gives some announcements about the end of the semester next week.

Then we have classes. We take turns reading out loud in English and French, then do some math. My desk group is great: Carrie is the best at math, Omar can draw amazing things, Yuki makes everybody laugh, and *je suis bilingue* as my stepdad and Hanna are from Québec. We all work together.

Note: Rory is using Canadian-English, so some of his terms are different to British-English, including:
elementary school = primary school
mom = mum
pants = trousers
oatmeal = porridge
class = lesson
vice-principal = deputy headteacher
semester = term
math = maths
recess = breaktime
grade = year
cookie = biscuit

Je suis bilingue: "I am bilingual". "Bilingual" means you can speak two languages fluently.

Carrie

Omar

Yuki

me

When the recess bell rings, we scramble back into our coats. If it's colder, like –25°C (–13°F), or it's snowing or raining, we play in the gym or in our classrooms. But when it's about –9°C (15°F) like today, we still get to go outside.

Next, we have Social Studies, and the 5th graders give presentations on dams and renewable energy. Did you know you can get electricity from rivers? It's useful having mixed grade classes because you learn a lot that you'll need to know for the next year.

Lunch time! Carrie and I brought lunch from home. I swap my cheese sandwich for her peanut butter one. She has cookies and I have grapes, and today we both have carrot sticks!

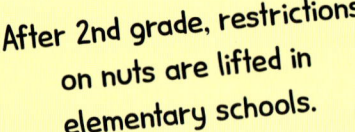

After 2nd grade, restrictions on nuts are lifted in elementary schools.

After lunch we go out to have a snowball fight with the rest of the 4th graders until it's time for afternoon classes. In Art class, we draw something from our art notebook, where we write interesting things we see during the week. Omar does an amazing pastel snowy owl. Did he really see an owl?!

Then we go to the Library Media Centre and work on our coding projects. There's an app where you drag and drop these little coding blocks and make games. I'm not really sure what my game is yet, but it's got bears and aliens. Then it's time to pack up!

At 3:25, the bell rings, and I meet my stepsister Hanna in the playground. Mom is at the gate wearing the biggest coat you've ever seen.

I get a snack when we get in, then sit down to do my homework. Hanna has guitar lessons after school today, but we usually do our homework together. When I'm done, Mom practices lacrosse with me in the garden until it gets too dark, while my stepdad makes dinner. Hanna joins us for a bit until my stepdad calls, "*À table!*" I'm starving!

"*À table!*" means that dinner is ready.

We have Québécois split pea soup with big chunks of bread. I'm tired by now, so I go to my room to read for a bit until it's time to sleep.

Québécois split pea soup

FORMING A COUNTRY

People first arrived in Canada somewhere between 30,000 and 12,000 years ago. They walked over glaciers and land bridges that once connected North America to Asia. For thousands of years, different communities lived on and **cultivated** the lands.

FASCINATING FACT!

The maple leaf flag became the national flag in 1965. The old flag included a small Union Jack from the UK, but Canada wanted something more uniquely Canadian.

Early societies

Early communities had different ways of living. The Haudenosaunee were farmers and hunters who lived in longhouses. Plains peoples like the Cree followed the migration of animals and lived in **teepees**. Coastal and island communities like the Haida relied more on fishing.

French and British colonisation

In the 16th century, French and British explorers arrived and made claims on the land. This led to much fighting between the French, British and Indigenous peoples, despite some alliances. Europeans also brought diseases like smallpox that were deadly to Indigenous peoples.

War and peace treaties

In 1609, Frenchman Samuel de Champlain began a war with the Haudenosaunee that lasted decades. In 1701, the Haudenosaunee and other Indigenous groups signed a **peace treaty** with France. Britain and France had also signed a peace treaty giving Britain power.

Joins and separations

In 1867, the colonies were joined into one federal union. This was the beginning of Canada as a country. The new government introduced the Indian Act, which allowed them to take land and freedoms from Indigenous peoples, and even separate children from their parents.

Modern Canada

Today, Canada is a **democracy** led by an **elected government**. There have been many reforms to the Indian Act to try to address the harms done. However, there is still a lot of ongoing dispute over land claims and rights for Indigenous peoples.

Teepee

Great Peace of Montréal

First Parliament of the new Dominion of Canada

RAVEN STEALS THE LIGHT

A long time ago, the world was shrouded in darkness.

It was dark, dark, dark. And back then, ravens were bright white.

The Raven decided he was sick of the darkness and flew off in search of light.

There it is! This greedy man has the light!

The Raven decided to steal it all for himself.

One day, while the old man's daughter was picking berries by the river...

...the Raven turned himself into a pine needle...

...and then a baby!

Though being a baby was sometimes boring...

...the old man treated him well, and he knew his plan would work.

The Raven waited until he was old enough to get what he wanted.

Box!

Box!

Box!

The Raven dropped the sun onto the ground and the whole world became light.

VISITING THE MAPLE FARM

Maple syrup is a big industry in Canada. More than 70 per cent of all maple syrup comes from Canada. Read this brochure persuading you to visit a maple syrup farm in Québec.

Dan's Sugar Shack

Are you mad about maple syrup? Have you ever wondered how it's made? Come and visit Dan's Sugar Shack to find out. We'll take you on a fascinating tour.

Did you know maple syrup comes from the sap of the maple tree? First on the tour, we'll show you how we tap the trees to drain out the sap. See how our simple yet effective system of tubes then takes the sap to the sugar shack.

Next, explore the ingenious sugar shack itself. Here, you'll discover how we turn sap into syrup. When it's raw, the sap is more water than sugar. Our experts use an evaporator to boil out just the right amount of water. Watch as the sap transforms into sweet amber syrup.

We'll finish the tour in the wonderful tasting room, where you'll enjoy sampling our products: fluffy pancakes and syrup, delicious maple sweets, and chewy syrup taffy. Grab a bottle of our finest syrup from the gift shop on your way out.

The best time to visit is February to April. This is when we have sugar weather: the prime conditions for harvesting sap. Stop by and be a part of the action!

Evaporator

Maple sap

Descriptive words
amber, best, chewy, delicious, effective, expert, fascinating, fine, fluffy, ingenious, prime, simple, sweet, wonderful

What you can do
discover, enjoy, explore, find out, learn, sample, take part, taste, tour, visit

Write your own brochure about a place of interest. It can be somewhere you know or you would like to visit.
What can you see there? What can you do? When is the best time to visit?

GLOSSARY

Agriculture The practice of farming.

Arctic The northernmost area of the world, closest to the North Pole.

Biodiversity Variety in plant and animal life.

Boreal forest Forests that grow in northern regions where temperatures are below freezing for at least half the year.

Colonisation The act of taking control of a land and settling by force, often displacing people who already exist there.

Conservation The preservation and protection of animals, habitats and ecosystems.

Cultivate Prepare land and grow crops.

Democracy A form of government in which the people in power are elected by the general population.

Ecological Relating to the environment and ecosystems.

Economic Related to money and the economy.

Ecosystem A community of plants, animals and other environmental factors that exist together with relationships and interactions that affect each other.

Elected government A government who was voted in by the people.

Erosion When wind, water, ice or other natural pressure wears away at rock.

Export Something sold from one country or region to another country or region.

Extinct Having died out and no longer existing.

First Nations One of three groups of Indigenous peoples of Canada recognised by the government (the others are Inuit and Métis).

Glacier A huge mass of slow-moving ice.

Habitat The natural home of an animal or plant species.

Hydroelectricity A form of renewable energy generated by water.

Indigenous people The earliest inhabitants of a land or those who inhabited a land before colonists arrived.

Industry A particular area or type of business. For example, the automobile industry refers to the manufacture and sale of vehicles.

Inuit One of three groups of Indigenous peoples of Canada recognised by the government (the others are First Nations and Métis).

Invasive species A species that is non-native to an area but that has been introduced to and colonised that area. They are usually harmful to their environments.

Métis One of three groups of Indigenous peoples of Canada recognised by the government (the others are First Nations and Inuit).

Mountain A high, steep landform.

Mountain range A group or chain of mountains, usually with a name.

Multiculturalism The presence of multiple cultures. This can also refer to support for the mixing and presence of multiple cultures.

Native Referring to a plant or animal that lives naturally in a place and has not been brought there.

Peace treaty A formal peace agreement intended to end a conflict.

Permafrost A layer of ground that is below freezing for at least two years straight.

Population The people or organisms who live in a certain area. It can also mean the number of people or animals that live in a certain area.

Prairies A large, flat area of grassland.

Progressive In favour of new ideas and concepts that help the public, like equality and welfare.

Québécois Coming from Québec.

Renewable energy Energy from a natural source that won't run out. This includes solar power, hydropower and wind power.

Rural Related to the countryside. A rural space is usually smaller and further out in the countryside than an urban town.

Secular Having no religion.

Teepee A tent made of animal hides draped over poles. It has a chimney at the top to let smoke out.

Urban Related to towns or cities.

INDEX

ACKNOWLEDGMENTS

The publisher would like to thank the following for their kind permission to reproduce their photographs:

(Key: a-above; b-below/bottom; c-centre; f-far; l-left; r-right; t-top)

Alamy Stock Photo: GRANGER - Historical Picture Archive 11clb, North Wind Picture Archives 37crb; **Dreamstime.com:** Aa5176 37cra, Ernest Akayeu 7cl, Olena Bardysheva 31b, Edgar Bullon 6, Natalia Chernyshova 5, Chase Clausen 14bl, Harry Collins 16cla, Dark1elf 18, 31cl, F11photo 30, 36, Foodio 27cla, Kaedeenari 36clb, Kazakovmaksim 17b, Tetiana Kozachok 33tl (br), 34–35b (stationery), Michel Loiselle 24, Lopolo 42cr, 43tr, Oleh Marchak 17tr, Mikedesign 20b, Monkey Business Images 21b, Nexusplexus 20t, Sergei Nezhinskii 37cr, Paper Trident 31t, Stan Parkh 4, Pictureguy66 14clb, Elena Pimukova 32–33b (family), 35tr, Alexander Raths 25tl, Showvector 28bl, 29b, Wally Stemberger 11cl, Ihar Suprenionek 37tr, VectorMine 11tr; **Shutterstock.com:** Africa Studio 27bl, Alonephotoshoot 14tl, Ansarphotographer 16bl, Sergei Bachlakov 19cl, BNP Design Studio 28tr, David Boutin 16tl, Martin Cloutier 43ca, Jim Cumming 13b, Chase D'animulls 9ca, daniellebra 22, Ian Duffield 14cla, Mercedes Fittipaldi 27tl, Jack Frog 25cl, Gorodenkoff 21t, GROGL 9cl, Incomible 32-33, 34-35, Javen 10, Lyudmyla Kharlamova 28cl, 29cl, 32tr, Aliaksei Kruhlenia 23cl, Lucky-photographer 7t, Erik Mandre 13tl, Pavel Mikoska 15tl, moloko_vector 9tr, 19tr, MuhammadIshfaq1 15cl, mutia_paint 26bl, Gergo Nagy 17cl, NatalyaBond 35br, nnnnae 24c, Juana Nunez 8, Natasha Pankina 6cra, 7b, 19cr, 20tl (br), 25tr, 42tr, 43br, pingebat 24br, Pixel-Shot 26, 37br, Pratico Media 27cl, Ondrej Prosicky 5tr, Anne Richard 15clb, Syed Ibad Rm 27clb, Pavlo S 4br, Scalia Media 12, senturkserkan 25bl, Jan Stria 16clb, Tehseen Photographer 15bl, ViDI Studio 19bl, Curtis Watson 13tr, Bing Wen 23t

Cover images: *front:* **Getty Images / iStock:** Nirut Punshiri t; **Shutterstock.com:** Sergii Figurnyi bl, Robert Vincelli br, Vincentuilll cr; *back:* **Dreamstime.com:** Kaedeenari cl; **Shutterstock.com:** David Boutin bl, Pavel Mikoska tl

All of the books in the *Super World* series have been reviewed by authenticity readers of the cultures represented.